LIFE'S ENCOUNTERS

MY STORY

Rev. Eve Axon

AuthorHouse™ UK
1663 Liberty Drive
Bloomington, IN 47403 USA
www.authorhouse.co.uk
Phone: 0800.197.4150

Published by AuthorHouse 10/31/2018

ISBN: 978-1-5462-9274-6 (sc)
ISBN: 978-1-5462-9273-9(e)

Print information available on the last page.

Any people depicted in stock imagery provided by Getty Images are models,
and such images are being used for illustrative purposes only.
Certain stock imagery © Getty Images.

This book is printed on acid-free paper.

Because of the dynamic nature of the Internet, any web addresses or links contained in this book may have changed
since publication and may no longer be valid. The views expressed in this work are solely those of the author and do not
necessarily reflect the views of the publisher, and the publisher hereby disclaims any responsibility for them.
Scriptures marked NKJV are taken from the NEW KING JAMES VERSION (NKJV): Scripture
taken from the NEW KING JAMES VERSION®. Copyright© 1982 by Thomas Nelson, Inc.
Used by permission. All rights reserved.

Scriptures marked NIV are taken from the NEW INTERNATIONAL VERSION (NIV):
Scripture taken from THE HOLY BIBLE, NEW INTERNATIONAL VERSION ®. Copyright©
1973, 1978, 1984, 2011 by Biblica, Inc.™. Used by permission of Zondervan

authorHOUSE®

CONTENTS

MY STORY 1

A WAR BABY 2

GROWING PAINS 6

HOSPITAL TREATMENT 7

DEEP WOUNDS 9

ROAD TO RECOVERY 10

MOVING ON 12

A STEP CHANGE 13

TAKING CONTROL 15

FINDING LOVE 18

A NEW LIFE TOGETHER 20

HEADING UP NORTH 22

SERVING GOD 24

FAMILY BUSINESS 31

AFRICAN LINKS 33

AROUND THE WORLD 41

BACK TO AFRICA 44

SPREADING THE WORD 46

HOME ROOTS 47

ABOUT THE FAMILY 50

PETS 51

ABSENT FAMILY 52

HEALING SCRIPTURES 53

THE AUTHOR 55

THE BOOK 56

BOOK DEDICATION

To Ron, my precious husband.

My eldest daughter Sue, her ex-husband Graham, their three children Lydia,
Heather and Harry, and Heather's son George, our great grandson.

My younger daughter Ruth and her husband Gustaf.

Those members of the family now in heaven.

Friends who have passed away, leaving husbands, wives and family.

To my special friends, Julie and Eileen, and daughter Sue, who helped me
with the proof reading and typing up of my memories.

My daughter, Ruth painted the picture of 'Geese in Flight', which is on the cover of my book.

My daughter, Sue painted the picture of the 'Single Rose', which is on the book dedication page.

MY STORY

Place of Birth: Dingle, Liverpool, 2 December 1942
Sister: Dorothy, aged five
Brother: Glynn, aged three, named after our Father
Me: Eva – I was named after my Mother
Dad was away at Dunkirk. He returned home in June 1942.
Mum worked as a cleaner and in a local bomb factory.

A WAR BABY

In 1945, we moved to Landford Place, Broadway, Liverpool. Dorothy, then aged eight, went to live with our grandparents in Dingle. I'm not really sure why, possibly so she could continue to attend the same school there. When Grandma died four year later, Dorothy then aged twelve, moved back into the family home.

In 1948, when I was five years old, I started at the local infant school. On my first day, I loved my school uniform, a grey tunic, white blouse, tie, blazer and black shoes. Because we were poor, Mum was able to use coupons to buy the uniform. It was the smartest outfit I had ever had.

I soon realised I was left-handed. This meant the teacher hit me across my knuckles with a ruler, so I soon learned to write with my right hand. I also realised another way I was different from other children in my class. In my insecurity, I had developed a bad stutter. We would stand and read a paragraph from a book. I loved reading but felt ashamed when asked to read aloud because of my stutter. The teacher just said, "Eva, its okay. Just sit down." I felt dismissed and inadequate, even though I knew I was great at reading.

Swimming became my next fear. At age four, I nearly drowned at a swimming pool on a day's outing to New Brighton. In my enthusiasm I ran and jumped into the adult pool instead of the children's one. There seemed to be no bottom and the sides were slippery, so I couldn't climb out. Luckily a man nearby saw me, pulled me out and did first aid, getting the water out of my stomach. He no doubt saved my life.

I always felt I was different from my Brother and Sister.

My Dad was badly scarred from being a soldier at Dunkirk and he turned to drink. When drunk, he either sang, "Heart of My Heart, I Love that Melody" or sobbed, over family members and friends who had died during the war.

In fact he himself had been feared dead. We'll never know what trauma he endured, but when he unexpectedly returned home from the army, the horror of war had deeply affected him. He screamed out in his sleep and suffered with his nerves. There was no help or support for soldiers coming back from the Second World War. He stayed in Dingle, Liverpool, for five years with Grandma and Grandad. I have no memory of Grandad. Gar—the name we called Gran—was diabetic and blind.

My Mum, believing Dad was not coming home, met a kind, caring man at the bomb factory. They intended to marry when the war was over. She became pregnant with me. Then Dad came home. So we became a family again. Although we grew up as a family unit, I always knew deep inside that I wasn't my Dad's child.

Mum worked in tough jobs in several different factories throughout her life. Dad worked at Bibby's down at the docks until he retired. Times were hard in those days.

Glynn, Eve & Dorothy (brother & sister family photo)

Ian & Denise (Dorothy's children in recent photograph)\

GROWING PAINS

My sister, Dorothy, was always there for me, especially at Christmas. She did a stocking with gifts inside. We always had one special toy. One year, Glynn had a Meccano set. He loved to build with it. He eventually became a car mechanic. He joined the RAF at nineteen. Later, he met his wife, Jessie, and had two children, a boy and a girl. They are still enjoying their lives together and now also have two beautiful grandchildren.

Dorothy married Don and they had two children. When Ian was three and Denise just a small a baby, Don was killed when his car went out of control on a patch of black ice. He died instantly but my sister never recovered from his death; it was a great shock to us all. He was a kind and loving husband, Father, and Son, taken away so unexpectedly at the start of his adult life.

I left school when I was fifteen and had various jobs. I worked as a chemist's assistant; at a drinks company in the transport office; making clothes at "Simon's Sewing Factory" for Marks and Spencer, who had very high standards. I have sewed most of my life. A natural gift which led to me becoming a seamstress and tailoress.

HOSPITAL TREATMENT

At nineteen, I had my appendix removed. The following year, 1962, I had a cyst removed from my left hand. And while in hospital this second time, I developed a strangulated hernia. I was very ill and nearly died.

A year later, I married a man I had met at church. We married at the Baptist church I attended on 23 March 1963. Sadly, our marriage did not last. Our Daughter Susan, was born on 26 April 1965. My husband worked at a power station in Staffordshire, and we moved into a flat provided by the company he worked for. Before we moved in, we lived with a woman who had lost her husband in the war. Things were very basic. She had a stone drum that you put coal under and had to light a fire to heat up water, a mangle for getting the water out of the clothes when doing the laundry, and an even more old-fashioned 1920s electric stove, to cook on. Not a great start to our married life as I felt alone and isolated. After us living in the flat for six months, we moved to a company house in Armitage, near Rugeley in Staffordshire.

Susan was born in Andressie Hospital in Burton on Trent, Staffordshire. She weighed five pounds seven ounces. She was tiny but gorgeous. After ten days of breastfeeding, I suffered from postnatal depression and was moved to another hospital for treatment. Initially, Susan could not be with me and, as my husband's parents had recently moved from Liverpool and now lived a few doors from us in Armitage, they were able to look after Susan.

I started to recover, but was still not able to return home, so Susan was brought to the hospital to be with me. I took care of her during the day, while the nurses did her feeds at night so I could sleep. Having her with me helped my recovery. My husband, because of his work commitments and the distance we lived from the hospital, was not able to visit.

DEEP WOUNDS

When I was well enough to return home, he and his parents suggested I should get a job. I worked as a clothes manager at a well-known supermarket in Rugeley. Although I enjoyed my job, I missed not spending more quality time with our daughter. I loved to sing "Jesus Loves Me" and read to her at bedtime. Susan was dedicated at a Baptist church in Lichfield when she was eight months old. I wanted to commit her life to God. I gave my heart to the Lord when I was eleven years old and prayer had always been important to me.

Our marriage began to fail. My Sister Dorothy, came to visit in 1968 when Susan was three years old. She saw how depressed I had become and took me back with her to Liverpool. Unfortunately, this meant I had to leave Rugeley without Susan, so she stayed with her Father and her paternal Grandparents.

Sometimes in life, we have to make difficult decisions. That was one of them. It changed my life and Susan's. We can't change the past, but lessons are learned that make us stronger and more able to face the future.

My sister was good to me. I lived with her and her children Ian, then seven years old, and four-year-old Denise. In 1968, I began divorce proceedings on the grounds of incompatibility. At that time, Susan still lived with my husband and his parents. I only saw her for a few hours every two to three months, with them present. It was a very difficult time for all involved.

ROAD TO RECOVERY

My divorce came through in 1969, and I was granted custody of our daughter, now nearly five. She joined me in the West Derby area of Liverpool, living with my sister and her children. The three children went to the local school. My husband came once a month to take Susan to stay with him and his parents Friday to Monday. During this time I worked in Liverpool as a sales assistant.

I decided to make a fresh start in 1971. Doris and Alan, friends from the church I attended, had moved to Beaconsfield with their three children. On a visit to see them, I opened up about my situation to them. They said Susan and I could move to Beaconsfield and stay with them until I was able to find employment, because I needed to secure a suitable job, ideally, a live-in position.

I applied for a position with a family who had three children—a baby ten months old, a four-year-old son, and a daughter aged six, the same age as Susan. The wife had a bad back meaning she struggled with looking after the children and her husband owned his own garage. My duties were to look after the children, take and collect them with Susan, from the local school, do the cooking, clean the house, and so on. At that time, I was also completing a typing course.

Susan and I had full board, but the husband was not willing to pay my insurance stamp, and I did not receive any wages. So, in the afternoons while the children were in school, I cleaned cars in a garage near their house, four rows of cars every day. It was winter, and it was hard, cold work. The owner of the garage gave me a job inside valeting cars, and a young lad cleaned the cars on the forecourt, much to my relief. I also had a radio to listen to.

On a lighter note, we went with the family on a short break to Morecambe, staying in a bed and breakfast. There was no kitchen in the bedroom, so after eating our food the first night, I placed the dirty dishes in a small sink to soak. The four children and I went to see synchronised swimming, whilst the parents went to a show. We enjoyed the evening very much. But when we went back to the bed and breakfast, we found water from the sink had overflowed and affected the flat below. A small payment was made and no further action was taken.

MOVING ON

When Susan went to stay with her Dad, I sometimes had the weekend off. I stayed with Doris and Alan, such great friends. I mentioned I was finding my situation difficult for Susan and myself, and they helped me look for a better position. In the local paper we saw a job with accommodation with a couple named Mr and Mrs Lane. They had a daughter at home, Victoria, who was six months younger than Susan. On the Sunday I went for an interview, I was given the position with board and a wage of five pounds a week. They had a granny flat for us to live in. This was in Windsor, not far from Beaconsfield. I worked my notice with the other family and then took up this new position.

Mrs Lane had two daughters at university from her first marriage, and Mr Lane had two sons from a previous marriage, also at university. During the summer holidays, they would come home and it was my responsibility to cook for them, wash their clothes, as well as cleaning the house. From time to time, I would help Mr Lane with his correspondence.

Mrs Lane had inherited investments from family relatives. The money left to her, was to buy property. So, as Mr Lane's business was in central London, they decided to buy a property in Walpole Street, Chelsea, London, intending for Sue and I to move with them. After viewing the property with the family, I didn't feel it was right for us to live in London. Mrs Lane was not pleased at my decision. They also bought a place in the New Forest, a large cottage. I saw it and was impressed with it but around this time Victoria was sent to boarding school, so it was time for me to move on. Mrs Lane was a lovely person to work for.

A STEP CHANGE

I was due to visit my friends for the weekend, as Susan was going to be staying with her Dad. While with them I saw an advert in the local church magazine for a position for an assistant to the warden of a Christian care home in Buckinghamshire - a care home for the elderly. So, on the Sunday afternoon I went for an interview which was with Mr and Mrs Williams and a lady called Mrs Peterson from the local Methodist Church, which part-funded the care home. The interview went well and they offered me the role.

Because I had Susan with me, we moved into a flat in the staff part of the care home, where Mr and Mrs Williams also lived. The flat had just two rooms, one bedroom for Susan and my room which was a studio room. But we had our own space at last and I could choose my own furniture, which I really enjoyed doing. I also had a small amount of disposable income for the first time, which I used to take driving lessons.

The home was quite small with 14 residents. My duties were to clean rooms, cook meals and other general house care, as required. The only staff were the Williams and myself, so we worked a 12 hour shift rota. Susan soon settled in at the local school. I passed my test and bought a car, which meant freedom to travel and life started to feel much better for me.

Another staff member joined us, Irene, who had recently finished Bible School. All was fine until one day, Irene asked for time off to visit her fiancé who was still at Bible School. She and Mr Williams had a disagreement about her request and things became a little heated. Consequently, the next day Mr Williams gave her the sack and left her cards on the table in the kitchen. She was so upset, she went to see Mrs Peterson. The situation was very difficult for all concerned as Mr Williams was not actually Irene's employer. As a consequence, Mr & Mrs Williams decided to leave and went home to Scotland. Irene went to stay with her fiancé.

TAKING CONTROL

I was asked to become matron by the Board. This was quite a challenge, so I asked for five additional members of staff – a part-time cleaner, cook, handyman/gardener, and two more carers. I was responsible for the day-to–day running of the home; buying the food, organising the shifts, managing the resident's payments and pensions, and the wages for the staff.

The residents were demanding but lovely and there was a calm and relaxed atmosphere. Because the home belonged in part to the local Methodist Church, the Reverend John Tynam would visit each Friday to spend time with the residents and give communion. I would join him in his prayers for each of them and he also prayed with the staff.

Each morning and evening the staff and I would have a time of prayer together, for God's help in our duties and for any residents who were unwell.

Personally, I was in a much better place with wages of £300 per year and full board for Susan and myself. Things ran to a steady and predictable timetable, giving a sense of structure we'd not previously had. We ate our meals at the same time as the residents in the staff kitchen just off the main dining room. There was also church on Sundays – any residents who wanted to go along were picked up by other church members and brought back for lunch, after the morning service.

Then in early 1973, Susan and I were invited to stay with a friend, Janet, who lived in Partington, Manchester. Janet suggested we stay with her for a weekend, as she lived with a church pastor and his wife who were due to be away on holiday, so she would be on her own in the house. We went along.

On the Sunday we attended the Baptist Church with Janet who introduced me to Ron, a deacon at the church. Some friends of my Sister also attended this Baptist church, Diane and Nathan. My sister had known Diane since her school days.

In conversation, I mentioned that Susan and I were going to stay in my Aunt's caravan in North Wales, and they realised they were booked in at a caravan site nearby, for the same week. So during the holiday their daughter stayed with Susan and I, and we spent the days at the beach together. They talked about the church deacon, Ron. I had liked him when we met, but I never expected to see him again.

Nimes. We stayed with the daughter and family of Rachel, who was in our Church Fellowship. We were there for two weeks during which, Ron taught in the Bible School.

The following year, we were invited by friends to Northern Ireland. We stayed with Jim Baldwin and family. They arranged meetings for us in Dungannon and Armagh. Their hospitality was wonderful and we really enjoyed preaching in their church. We were also invited to family homes for morning or afternoon tea. Through this, we received several invitations to return to Ireland.

In 1986. Ron was interviewed for the Pastorate at the Baptist church in Bacup in Lancashire, by a man named Ralph Fisher. When we went for the interview, we were told no house was available to move into, as the previous Pastor and his family had gone to be missionaries in Brazil and the Manse had been passed to a letting agent and was currently rented out. We prayed and said to God that if it was His will for us to move to Bacup, he would need to provide us with somewhere to live. Much to our surprise, we received a phone call from Ralph a few days later to say the house was now empty, as the family who were occupying the property had been using the garage to store stolen goods and had left overnight -a rather hasty retreat to get away from the police. So, when could we move in?

We went to view the house and soon realised there was no way of knowing which furniture belonged to the Pastor and which had belonged to the tenants. Our furniture was once again in storage. A few days before we moved, a letter came from the family saying they wanted their bed back! The drawers underneath it contained their personal belongings. This we were able to arrange.

We retired from leaders the Baptist church in 1987, but stayed on as members. Pastor Keith and Bridie and their two sons, who also lived in Bacup, took over the Pastorate and we worked closely with them and became good friends. They later moved to Scotland to pastor and sadly, Keith lost his life to cancer in 2016, aged 72. We still meet up with Bridie regularly. She sold their house and moved into a flat in Burnley. We all miss Keith who was a wonderful pastor, family man and friend to many in England and Scotland.

Sue & Graham (from wedding in 1985)

Heather & Simon (from wedding in 2014)

Heather & Simon with son George (winter family photo in 2016)

Lydia & James (from wedding May 2017)

Gustaf,Ruth, Sue & Fiona (taken at Lydia & James wedding)

FAMILY BUSINESS

Around this time, our elder daughter Susan married Graham, who she had met while studying in Bristol. They were married in the Church of the Good Shepherd on a bright, brisk December day and settled in Bristol where they still live.

On 13 May 1986, our first grandchild, Lydia was born and two years later, on 14 May 1988, her younger Sister, Heather. Sue and Graham decided to try one more time to see if they could have a son to join Graham at Chelsea football matches - and Harry was born on 7 April, 1990.

Heather is now married to Simon and our first great grandchild was born in October 2016. He is called George. Lydia married James on 19 May, 2017. Harry is currently living in London, trying to set up his own business in event management.

Ruth, who is 10 years younger than Sue, attended Liverpool University and her studies included Science, Medicine and Health. In 2000, Ruth went to the African School of Missions. Besides doing Religious Studies, she worked as a nurse in the local township clinic, mostly advising women on health issues linked to AIDS. It was here she met Gustaf and in December 2002 Ruth and Gustaf were married. Gustaf and his best man wore blue waistcoats and dickie bows. After a short period of time, they came to England and settled in Liverpool. Ruth has continued in the Public Health Service and will soon complete her doctorate. In 2016, Ruth and Gustaf took over the pastorate of Victory Life Centre in Liverpool.

Gustaf & Ruth (at their wedding in South Africa)

AFRICAN LINKS

Back in 1965, while I was living in Staffordshire, I attended a Pentecostal church. I had a close relationship with a couple called Joan and Harold, who had a daughter named Dawn and a son called Roger. They were very good to me. Around the time I moved to my Sister's in Liverpool, they left for South Africa, to become missionaries. I continued to write to Joan and, after many invitations from them, we finally went out to stay with them. Our visits ran over ten years from 1989 up until 1999 – six visits in total.

Our first trip was for a holiday. They lived in Johannesburg and worked in the townships, doing soup kitchens for the unemployed and preaching in the churches. They took two weeks holiday during our visit to show us around, including an amazing safari into Kruger National Park, where we saw elephants, lions and tigers in their natural environment. It was a wonderful experience. There were fantastic waterfalls. We also met with their friends and family members in Durban. On later visits, we preached in different churches. By then, their children were married with families of their own.

In 1990, on a visit to a house church in Hebden Bridge we met, a Nigerian called Segan Oshinaga who was preaching there. We got talking with Segan and he invited us to go to Nigeria. So we went, later that year. Pastor Segan arranged meetings for us in Benin City, Ibadan and Lagos. We preached to large crowds and many came for prayer after the meetings. It was an amazing sight to see and listen to a thousand people singing hymns together.

During our time in Ibadan, we were asked to pray for a woman in the pastor's office who was in terrible pain with a back problem. She was in too much pain to attend the church service, so arrangements were made for us to see her in the office the day after one of the evening services. The lady ran a business making and selling clothes and she was afraid she might have to sell her business due to her on-going back problems. So, we prayed with her for God to heal her back and said "Goodbye". To our delight she returned the next day, free from pain, having been totally healed by the Lord. As thank you gifts for our prayers, she gave Ron and I a beautiful set of African style clothes.

For our last Sunday service in Ibadan, we thought it would be a nice gesture to wear these African clothes. To our astonishment, all the congregation were dressed in Western style clothes. They gave up a loud cheer as we stepped onto the preaching platform, pleased that we had identified ourselves with them.

That evening, the praise and worship was long and intense and there was a long queue of people waiting to be prayed for after the service. It took about 3 hours to pray with them all as they refused to go home until they had received the gift of prayer. It was a powerful experience and we saw some people healed instantly as a result of their faith in the power of God, and of our prayers.

The cultural difference between this part of the world and ours back home in Northern England was stark. So many people in extreme poverty. Young and old beg on the streets. Crime and mugging's of foreigners are frequent, so we travelled in taxis and stayed in various secure hotels, but the pastors, leaders and people we met, were all very gracious towards us.

Our next visit to Nigeria was two years later and we met Pastor Louis and preached in his church in Ibadan. He invited us to stay for three weeks. During this time we met a lovely young man called Frank and his wife Abiose. Frank had a wonderful gift of being able to work with young people. It was such a pleasure to stay and minister at the large university campus where their ministry was focussed, in Ibadan. The young people were eager to embrace Christianity and receive salvation. Frank later came to the UK and stayed with us – at this time we were living in Colne, in Lancashire.

Shortly afterwards, we received the sad news that Frank had died in a road accident. We were told he had bought a car which turned out to have faulty brakes. There was no MOT test in Nigeria so vehicles can have unseen problems. Frank, with three of his friends in the car, had ended up crashing into a river. Frank and one friend Ezekiel, survived the crash but, the couple in the back seat died at the scene. Both Frank and Ezekiel were in hospital with bad injuries for some time and Frank never recovered. It seems he felt responsible for the deaths of his friends. He left behind a lovely wife and young daughter. We never went back to Nigeria, although we have special memories of our two visits.

Eve & Ron (taken at Clayton-Le-Moors Baptist Church 2005)

Eve (at Bowland Street Mission 2018)

Ron preaching (at Bowland Street Mission 2018)

Ron (taken in the garden)

Family Pets Kayleigh (the cat). Sophie (our previous cat)
Annie (our pet dog who passed away September 2018

AROUND THE WORLD

In 1991, Ron went to East Germany on a preaching tour for two weeks with a friend called Daniel. They stayed in Jena, with another friend, Alex who arranged various meetings for them. This was not long after the fall of the Berlin wall and East Germany still resembled how other parts of Europe had been in the fifties, with large factories and smoking chimneys. Daniel spoke good German and this helped the conversation to flow with those they met, so they had good services and met many lovely German Christians.

The following year, Ron and I were invited to America by Pastor John Richie. He arranged meetings in Pennsylvania and Kansas and he, with his elders, took us to a conference where he had arranged for us to be ordained as Ministers, with the laying on of hands. For me, it was a truly memorable occasion. I also remember that after one of the early Morning Prayer meetings, Pastor John and two of the church elders took us out for breakfast - the food portions in America were amazing and it was probably the largest breakfast I've ever had. We met some lovely people on this trip and it was a great country for us to minister in.

The next trip for Ron was in 1993, when he went to Kenya for two weeks with another Pastor, Jason Richards. Similar to when we were in Nigeria, they preached to large crowds at both outdoor and indoor church services.

Closer to home, our second visit to Northern Ireland was also that year, when we stayed with Pastor Graham and Harriet Aldcroft, who arranged a number of services for us to preach at.

Then in 1994, we went on our second visit to South Africa. This time Joan and Harold arranged the church services for us. We also went to Durban to visit their daughter Dawn, her husband and two teenage sons.

We also returned to South Africa the following year as earlier in the year, Pastor Harold and Joan had received the sad news that Shane, their grandson, had died suddenly aged just 19. He had been running with his girlfriend and on returning home, had taken a shower, but then collapsed and died. He passed away in his girlfriend's arms. It transpired a virus had attacked his heart. We stayed there for two weeks and tried to bring some comfort, during this sad time for the family.

In 1995, we went back to Northern Ireland for a further visit with Pastor Graham Anderson. We preached at a church near the border called 'Mountain Lodge', where in 1990 four of the church elders had been shot in an IRA terrorist attack - all four had died. We spent time with the wives and their families, who demonstrated such grace and forgiveness. In a bitter twist of fate, Pastor Graham had been in hospital at the time of the shooting and as he was also an elder at that Church. It undoubtedly saved his life, as he would otherwise have been there that evening. We also visited an ex-soldier who was one of a group of three that were attacked while driving along a country road. His two colleagues died. It was a car bomb device. After the explosion he said he looked down and saw his leg was hanging off. He prayed "God, if you save my life, I'll serve your forever". His leg could not be saved and he had to overcome the loss of his fellow soldiers, but since that day, he and his family serve the Lord. His is just one of the many courageous stories we heard from the people we met during this visit.

In 1996, Pastor Maurice Miles and his wife invited us to preach with them in Ecuador. We were there for three weeks. Pastor Miles was in charge of two churches, so we preached in both. As neither of us speak much Spanish we used an interpreter and were intrigued when rather than introducing us as Ron and Eve, it was Ronaldo and Evita, quite a nice ring to it, we thought! We met many lovely people and several received prayer from us for various needs. And our Spanish improved enough for us to go shopping.

Later that year, we went back to Ireland for two weeks. This time Pastor Graham arranged meetings for us in different areas, including Dungannon and Armagh. Once again the generous hospitality bestowed on us by the people we met was wonderful – in particular the ladies of Armagh made the most delicious sandwiches and cakes.

Our trip in 1997 was on the opposite side of the planet. Through "International Gospel Outreach" we had made contact with a couple called Donald and Janet who lived in Melbourne, Australia. We were invited to go there for five weeks to speak at a number of church services and they also took us to visit some of the World's places of outstanding natural beauty.

We returned the next year and spent time with Pastor Jack Bloomfield, the President of International Gospel Outreach, in Australia. He took us to minister at a place called Lightening Ridge, an opal mining area. It was quite an experience, as we stayed in a warehouse with fourteen other people and as many children. If you went to the bathroom at night, there were lots of creepy crawlies. During the day, it was very hot, to say the least. We only manged to stay four days. The Pastor had encouraged his people to buy a plot of the Opal mine which he and the church leaders arranged to be mined and they then sold the opals to raise funds for the church. The mines were very deep and dangerous. It was not a nice place and I have to admit I wanted to leave after the first night. Pastor John also took us to several other churches and fellowships, so it was an interesting trip, in all.

BACK TO AFRICA

In 1999, we visited Joan and Harold in South Africa again. While we were there, their daughter, Dawn, was diagnosed with breast cancer. She refused treatment and sadly the cancer progressed very quickly and she passed away aged just 42. It was another very sad time for Harold and Joan who had now lost both their daughter and their grandson.

During this visit, we ministered at a community centre in Thembisa Township, where there was a positive response to the Gospel message. After spending two weeks in Cape Town, we returned to the Johannesburg area and made a second visit to Thembisa. After the sermon, Harold said to Ron "Let's go to the car and bring back some sweets for the children". They made the mistake of leaving the building before the rest of the people. On walking to the car, Ron and Harold were ambushed by three men with combat knives. They were robbed of money and bank cards. They might have been injured but for the congregation starting to come out of the community centre. On seeing the crowd, the robbers fled. Two weeks before we had flown out to South Africa, we had seen a TV documentary about Thembisa being a very dangerous place, so it came as no surprise. But we had trusted in the Lord for protection and firmly believe that without it, the situation could have turned out to be much worse.

In 2000, we were back in South Africa but this time we went to the African School of Missions in White River. Our daughter, Ruth, was there studying Health and Women's Issues. She spent part of her time there working in the local township clinic, which was both challenging and fulfilling. She was working as a palliative nurse with young mothers who were dying of AIDS. It was while she was working here that Ruth met Gustaf and they married later that year, at a lovely service in White River. Sue and her family joined Ron and I at their wedding.

In 2003, unfortunately we received the news from Joan that Harold had died. We miss our friends very much, as that was the last time we went to South Africa.

SPREADING THE WORD

In 2004, Reverend Jack Bloomfield invited us to go back to Australia. We were there for six weeks preaching in different locations, and we also spent some time in Brisbane. And in 2005, we went back to America, preaching in a church in Pittsburgh. Here we met a lovely church elder called Drew Osmund, who invited us to join a barbeque with his family. We also visited a young persons' home for disabled people and spent time with a young man who was a wheelchair user. His attitude to living positively with his disability was both inspiring and courageous, and made a lasting impression on both Ron and I.

We travelled to many different countries over a period of 20 years. It gave us the opportunity to share of God's love and forgiveness in all four countries within the United Kingdom, in France, Germany, the USA, Ecuador, Nigeria, Kenya, South Africa and Australia. It was an honour and a privilege to serve Him in this way and hopefully to touch the hearts of the many wonderful people we met and shared experiences with.

HOME ROOTS

Between1990 and 2000, we lived in Colne, Lancashire and attended the "New Life Christian Centre". It was led by Pastor Gordon Barrett and his wife, Shelly. Ron was part of the team of preachers at this Christian Fellowship and I was mainly involved with the women's meetings. George White, who was also a member of this Church, owned an end of terrace house in Brown Street West, which we rented from him. We enjoyed living in Colne and being involved at this church.

In 1998, I rented a small shop just off Colne High Street where I sold wedding dresses, bridesmaids' dresses, and mums' outfits. I also worked as a seamstress making some bridal wear to order. Occasionally, I also made wedding cakes and did flower arrangements.

In 2000, our landlord had to sell the house for personal reasons, so we decided to see if we could find somewhere to rent near Skipton in North Yorkshire. We were visiting a local pastor and his wife, Patrick and Joyce Evans who showed us a newspaper advertising properties. There was one in the village of Carleton-in-Craven, just outside Skipton so, we phoned up to inquire about it. To our surprise, the owner, Paul Harrison, said he could be there for us to see the house in twenty minutes. The location was about ten miles north of Colne, but we jumped in the car straightaway and headed over.

We still live in this house, and after 17 years we are still very happy there. Our landlord, lives in New Zealand and he kindly made an agreement with us that he would keep the rent reasonable, if we did the repairs and upkeep to the property. Over the years we have made various improvements, and added features which will improve the value, should Paul decide to sell it. I closed the shop in Colne, shortly after we moved to Carleton. When we moved to Carleton, we decided to move to a church in Skipton too.

So, we pastored Clayton-le-Moors Baptist Church for six years. Ron still goes there to preach once a month when their Pastor has a Sunday off. The leaders are, a lady Pastor and 5 church elders who have been faithful servants to the church and its congregation, over many years. They are all special people with tender hearts full of love and compassion. During the last six years, we've seen some very dear friends pass on to Heaven, it includes the treasurer, Anne, Margaret, Edmond and Susan the church secretary. All these saints are now at rest with Jesus. They worked for Him on earth and their lives and testimonies live on in the hearts of those who worked with them.

I have had various jobs, working at Edinburgh Woollen Mill shop as a sales assistant, Johnson's the Cleaners as a tailoress and a local supermarket on the tills, plus at Rackhams, in the Planet Dress Department and also in the café. Above all, I prefer to work as a carer, including when I worked at Carleton Craven Care Home. I currently work for another care agency, looking after a lovely lady called Eileen. In addition, I also care for a neighbour Valerie, an arrangement made through her daughter, who lives in Lincoln. Valerie is also a pleasure to care for.

Ron's last job before he retired, was working at clothing retailer's, in the warehouse. It meant getting up at 5.30am but he arrived home after the shift ended at three in the afternoon, which had some merit. Overall he didn't really enjoy the pressure of needing to achieve difficult targets, so it was good he was able to do it until he retired.

On 2 December 2012, I celebrated my 70th birthday with a surprise party, organised by Ron, Sue and Ruth. It was held at a stately home near Gargrave, North Yorkshire. Ron told me we were going out for a surprise meal with two friends, Valerie and Pat. When we arrived, there was a large group of family and friends, who began to sing "Happy Birthday", as we walked through the door. I was presented with many lovely cards and gifts from those there and from friends who had not been able to join us. It was a very special occasion!

In 2014, we decided to visit "New Life" church in Thornton, near Bradford, as a close friend was attending there and had said good things about it. We received a very warm welcome from the Pastor and his wife and we still attend there, when we are not preaching in other churches. Ron has been a tutor in the Bible School there for the last three years. He also preaches quite often on Sunday mornings. The church is nineteen miles away from where we live, so it's a bit of a drive, but it's always worth the trip as we have many friends there and enjoy the fellowship.

Recently, we have also joined a Church in Settle and help with the ministry there from time to time. Pastor Tony, and his wife Denise, belong to International Gospel Outreach, which is the movement Ron and I belong to and the one that took us around Australia, so we have plenty in common.

ABOUT THE FAMILY

From 2016, Ruth, and Gustaf, have been pastoring a church in Liverpool. The church is in the Norris Green area, close to where I went to school. The church is called "Victory Life", and the building where they are now, is for their own specific use. Previously, they shared a Church of England building. Having sole use, means they are able to arrange various services and activities to support the local community. Ruth also has a full-time job in Public Health and is nearing the end of her doctorate studies.

Susan is now divorced from Graham and still lives in Bristol as do our granddaughters and their husbands, and our great-grandson, George. Susan has a management position with a well-known banking group.

PETS

Over the years, our family has enjoyed having pets. Back in the seventies Sue asked to have a cat, so we got Sophia, a tabby, from the Rescue Centre. Later, we also had a dog called Prince, a mongrel. Prince lived until he was fourteen but then had problems with his rear legs and other complications. Sophia lived to be sixteen and then due to kidney problems, she also had to be put to sleep. When we lived in Colne we took in Kayleigh through the Cat's Protection League. She also lived until she was sixteen.

More recently, we went to the Dog's Trust in Leeds and chose Annie, a Staffy-cross. We had some fun times enjoying her sweet and lovely nature before she passed on last year. We have had great pleasure from our pets and will always miss each one. Life goes on. Ron and I have had 43 years of married life with plenty of trials and many rich blessings.

ABSENT FAMILY

Our parents and other members of our families should be mentioned as they are no longer with us, starting with Ron's immediate family.

Dad, Charlie passed away 1970, aged 46.
Mother, Irene, passed away 2002 aged 72.
Step-dad, John, passed away 1988 aged 58.
Brother-in-law, Paul, passed away 2011 aged 64.
Ron has a brother Barry and a sister, Denise.
Ron's granny was a big influence on his life. She was Emily Smith, and passed away 1982, aged 95 and his grandad, Sidney, passed away in 1969, aged 75.
My immediate family were as follows:
Dad, Glynn, passed away in 1989 aged 79.
Mother, Eva, passed away in 1991 aged 81.
Sister, Dorothy, passed away in 2014 aged 79.
I also have a brother, Glynn who is married to Jessie.

HEALING SCRIPTURES

Hearing God's Voice

I Samuel 3 v 1-10 v10 The Lord spoke to Samuel – Samuel answered "Speak Lord for your servant hears you."

Trusting in the Lord

Proverbs 3 v 5-6 "Trust in the Lord with all your heart, and lean not on your own understanding. In all your ways, acknowledge Him and He shall direct your paths."

The Lord Protects

Psalm 91 v 2, 4,11,15,16 v2 "The Lord is my refuge and fortress, my God in whom I trust. v4 "His faithfulness will be your shield …"

v11 "He will command his angels concerning you, to guard you in all your ways."

V15-16 "Because he loves me," says the Lord, "I will rescue him. I will protect him. Call upon me, I will answer. I will deliver him and honour him. With long life will I satisfy Him."

The Lord watches over us

Psalm 121 v 1,2,5,7,8 v1-2 "I will lift up my eyes to the hills, where does my help come from? My help comes from the Lord, the maker of heaven and earth."

V5 "The Lord watches over you, the Lord is your shade at your right hand."

V7-8 "The Lord will keep you from all harm. He will watch over your life. The Lord will watch over your coming and going, both now and for evermore."

All these Scriptures are particularly relevant to my life. At age 11, I prayed to hear God's voice. I attended a Church in Liverpool where truth from the Bible was taught. I also studied the Bible myself, asking for help and guidance, trusting in God's faith fullness. Knowing His love and support through the difficult times, helped me to rest in His love. The Lord guides us through the Bible. He rescues, protects and answers prayer.

THE AUTHOR

I was born in Liverpool during the Second World War. I was the youngest of 3 children. When I was 5 I started school. My uniform was purchased with coupons as we were still on rations. I enjoyed school, although being left-handed was not acceptable. Have the ruler across my knuckles, I soon learned to write with my right hand.

I left school at 15 and had various jobs until I moved to Rugeley in Staffordshire, aged 20. Susan was born 2 years later. After problems in the marriage, I was divorced when Susan was 3. I moved back to Liverpool to live with my sister. I later moved to Beaconsfield. Needing accommodation with my job, I worked with 2 different families and later became matron of a residential home for the elderly.

During a visit to Manchester, I met Ron at his Church. We married 6 months later and have a daughter, Ruth.

Ron and I have pastored 3 Churches and ministered in 8 countries outside the UK.

THE BOOK

This book is a reflection of many changes in my life.

My father was in Dunkirk and returned home just before I was born. He suffered from PTSD as a result of what he experienced in the war. No emotional support was given to returning service personnel, after the war.

From leaving school to this present time, we have moved house several times due to changes in circumstances. We have rented privately over 44 years. Some residencies were short-term, others for several years. Our 2 daughters went to at least 11 schools each. They have made great achievements, in their academic and working lives, of which we are proud. During my working life, I have been a dress maker and tailoress. I have enjoyed my position of carer to the elderly. Prayer is important in my life.

THE END

Printed in the United States
By Bookmasters